Beautiful Heart

A collection of heartfelt poems

By Madlyn Epstein Steinhart

the three
tomatoes
The Three Tomatoes Book Publishing

Dedication

Simply The Very Best
Meryl
Tony
Vivian
Jeanette
Leslee
Sori
Rita
Dr. Ellen

and my WPIA Howie

Table Of Contents

Heart Burn... 57

Beautiful Heart

Beautiful Heart

If this applies to you then bravo
You are not a member of the piranha pool
Corruptive liars stuck in yesterday
How they function today is a question for sages?
Religion and politics aside
What was was
What is is
How about common sense?
How about being a human being and not a monster?
How about listening and not commenting?
People cry out on social media
Their words not worth reading
Insult to injury
We all bleed red blood
We all cry tears
We have all lost and been in pain
We have dealt with so much and some have to learn
to deal
It is not easy
Not sleight of hand
You get real and appreciate what you have
Beautiful heart
Beautiful heart
Doing the very best we can
Expecting nothing in return but to be there and extend
a hand
Not wondering what is in it for me or you

When You Come Full Circle

When you come full circle
Revolving doors can be painful
Watch for sharp corners that might deter you
That includes people and places too
Others lurk where you least expect them
Shut the doors behind you for those who stayed a while,
but their time is up
They no longer play a role in your life
Be grateful they were there at all
Take that deep breath
You earned it
It took a lot out of you to reach this intersection and
plateau
You crossed it
Know that you did, but don't revel in it for too long
It served its purpose and down the road it will be a
private smile that only you will recognize
Just remember this when you come full circle
You now know what matters the most, so take care
of yourself
Those that will always be there for you are in reach
even when you are out of touch
Just look over your shoulder
As well as into your heart
When you come full circle

Sapphire Dancer

Nasty dismal overcast day with rain on and off
Then this little one appeared on a tall tree
In blue finery, bopping, tapping, fluttering and
shimming
A dancing solo
Bravo little dynamo
Take a bow
You made a gray day sunny and bright
Sapphire Dancer

Does A Tree Make A Sound When It Falls In The Forest?

Do the trees sigh?
Does the wind cry?
Do they gather to remember the loved one or friend
and say goodbye?
Was it a fire caused by a careless human, an architect,
was it sick
and Mother Nature called it home or to let go?
What happened to the tree when it was young, strong,
and tall long ago?
How many creatures scurried across its arms
to play or hide food?
Find shelter?
Was it maple, an oak, a redwood?
Maybe a ponderosa pine?
Did maple sap run from it or apples grow for all to see?
Does a tree make a sound when it falls in the forest?
Did an eagle rest on its branches and then take flight?
Next time, we'll have to get to know a tree better and
perhaps
we'll do more than ask questions about our
Dear Departed friend, tonight.

Caesar's Garden

You don't want to deal with imaging and hospitals
Whether patient or visitor
There is a nirvana in one
Breezes caress the sunshine
Counted the bird houses
Numbered seven
Mother Nature's son keeps it blooming filled with
peace, tranquility and greenery
He tends to his garden
Reminding you to take it easy
You can hear the collective sigh as you take it in
It sweetens the soul as a sanctuary should
Will wild turkeys come by?
Will the skunk grace you with his or her presence?
This precious oasis in the little utopia
A little piece of Walden
Thoreau would approve of
Caesar's Garden

Golden Lady

Her green and gold leaves flow like Rapunzel's
on this mild December day
You could almost climb those tresses
She welcomes the blue jays as they find a seat
on her limbs
She sways on the breeze and watches cars and shoppers
around her
Hope they stop to notice just how lovely she really is
Thanks for letting me get to know you

Gem

She is here
A miraculous gift for her family to treasure and adore
Challenging to have her join the party as her daddy
would say at this time in our world
It is a testament of just how much her parents love
each other
They love you more than any poet could express, even
your aunt
You shine unlike any other
Uncut and beautiful with a quality and luster all
your own
May the world welcome your arrival and be gentler,
kinder, and more caring for you.
As your begin your story filled with sunshine,
warmth and glory
May good health and joy surround you every moment
Welcome to the world, Little Gem

Sunshine

He is only two but commands smiles and awes
Every word he utters is a diamond because it is pure
and clear
His actions are vivid and innocent but wiser than
some adults
In fact, he simply makes more sense than they do
His fascination and joy is captivating
Just one look and he captures your heart and casts
a spell
This magical rebel
My Sunshine
He has my heart and gratitude

Lola Rae

Bright blue sky dotted with rainbow colored balloons
The look in your beautiful sapphire eyes when a puppy
or dog approaches
Every single moment should be precious for you
You have given us hope and magic
How has a year come and gone since we were graced
with your birth
and the gift of you?
The best event in 2020 was you!
So if you are sassy and have chutzpah then the world
beckons.
Happy first birthday on May 20!
Be happy and healthy our sweet Gem

Watching You Dream

You are peacefully napping
Wondering if your dreams are pleasant
Where will you wander and travel?
Revisiting the past
In touch with the memory of those you have lost
So when those blue eyes open
Quietly, I will await you.
Sleep well baby

New Love Song

There is no number high enough
And if there were it still would never explain the love
we share
So no matter the hurdle
So no matter the delay or interruption
So no matter the storm
We weather it
Stronger
Everlasting
Confident
So incredibly sure
My love, this is your new love song
with every beat of my heart

How Much Love

How much love does it take to find a strength that you never thought you possessed?

How much love does it take to say that scaling Everest naked would not be a challenge because it would be done for you?

How much love does it take when a parent hates your beloved and reminds you for the rest of your life even though you are incredibly happy together, but favors your sibling's spouse over yours?

How much love?

There will never be enough and whatever I can do to show you and share with you, you have my heart Babe!

How much love the number has not been invented yet and once it is

It will never be high enough

Everyday Is Valentine's Day

Never expected you to come into my life
Not the expecting type, more like the accepting type
We were not looking but we found each other on
September 14, 1979
Sharing dreams on the Belt Parkway
Many have come true and look forward to more
New York City sprinkled magic around us
Gently and quietly something special started
Everything just fell into place nicely and easily
Stars sparkled and realigned
You understand me better than I do myself
You still do
We jumped hurdles and healed broken hearts
Still working on those in progress
No matter what, no matter when, where, no matter who
No matter
We climb mountains slowly and steadily
Every moment for the rest of our days
Whispers and hugs will calm the tears in the middle
of the night
It always ends up better and alright
Everyday is Valentine's Day because you are my
best friend and love of my life
No greater gift, my love

When You Love Someone That Much You Do It

You are supposed to take care of yourself first before
you assist someone else
What if you are not able or you can't because what
they require
Only you can provide or give
Even when it is against your better judgement or what
you really want
You put yourself second
It is what it is
No matter what you think or say
When you love someone that much you do it
Having a good heart isn't always easy

It Is The Only One

Make it genuine
Make it divine
Make it the way you want it to be
Think of Dexter the dog from Colorado and you can do
the unthinkable
Many people were touched and moved by the dog who
lives the think I can spirit and does it
Realize the costs and the moments are precious and
must be seized
Sometimes it isn't pretty
Sometimes it isn't fair
Sometimes it is what it is doesn't apply
It's the only one
It's yours
Have at it
Taste it and revel in it
It's the only one
Just be kind and caring

Cape Cod Hydrangea Festival

Gentle moxie
Lush
Plush
Puffy clouds in a blue sky
Explosion of color
Even though we didn't attend but hope to down
the road
They like time and shade
Particular as to home and how they are watered
They are adored
After all we have been through and gone through
Nice to know that hydrangeas bring comfort and joy
They make you smile

Gentle Forest Vibrant Universe

Onyx trees viewing the shades gently exploding and
aligning above them as if reaching out
Crepe, flamingo, lemonade, rose, taffy
and watermelon pinks headed towards a star
Admiral, azure, lapus, navy and sky blues with
touches of diamond and lightning
dancing in the sky

My Heart Is Always With You

She sings of holding my hand beautifully
Bravo Stephanie, her real name
I will give up what I need to care for you
Not much I need any way
My heart is always with you
There are a very special few
There is so much more I can share and do
My heart is always with you
My heart is always with you

It's All About The Words

If you think then wake up at 2 am and try not to wake
anybody because that whisper woke you up
You are walking and you hope you have a pen or cell
phone nearby to jot an idea down
You are driving and Alexa isn't cooperating even
though she usually does
Artificial intelligence might help us out when our input
and output don't jive
You're flying and you almost miss the fasten your
seat belts call for landing
Been there and done that?
It's all about the words at least for me

Creating

Words and images for me
are interchangeable
Have always spoken to me in my head
Urging me to write them down and remember them
So I befriended them and besides being constant
companions
They are there for me
They remind me to keep creating
Not sure where we are going but go we shall

Changing Hearts And Minds

Bigotry
Narrow mindedness
Ignorance
This trio is beyond comprehension
Remember some will never change
Never saying never lightly
My wish is that changing hearts and minds
is the way we all should live
Yesterday and history need to be revisited
and accepted
Moving forward is up to everybody

Magic

Leo Sunshine
Lola the Gem
Hugging
Dancing
Playing
Happy to be in a family
Two first cousins growing up together
Magic

Pirouette And Pivot

Not planned
Not executed with precision exactly
5-6-7-8
You did the ball changes even when your spirit and soul
had other plans
You didn't let those dark clouds interrupt sunny days
Cyphering with strangers and friends from a distance
but together
Almost syncopated rhythm
The dynamics and focus were new to you
Your pivoting was freestyle with a musicality that you
didn't know you possessed
So switching lines and transitions were made to look
easy even though they never were
Take a bow and come shining thorough
Pirouette and Pivot no matter life's curve

Precious Time

Listen to the silence
You can still hear the tears falling
The cries that go unanswered
The selfishness that is killing Mother Nature and her
children
Softly but way too quickly
The majesty and the harmony is slowly fading
Precious time is slipping away
Help Mother Nature and her children before they
become a memory
What was isn't going to be much longer

Heart Ache

Stop Stepping On My Heart

I wear my heart on my sleeve
Sorry that you can't deal with that
Stop stepping on my heart
My words are measured and carefully thought through
Just how high and mighty are you?
Stop stepping on my heart
You are who you are
I am who I am
Let's not pretend anymore
Stop stepping on my heart
Tired of healing from yesterday's scars

It Is Time

Wish you had showed me about family
Told me of them
Welcomed them
Had you let go of issues and taught me about our
ancestors when you were here
Those I have come to know wish we could turn
back time
Grow up together
Know us as children
Been there and around us when you were taken from us
so early
We have a large family
It is time for me to know the people you never shared
with me
The reasons no longer matter
You would have turned 95 tomorrow
With your children, sons in-law, grandchildren,
great grandchildren, and your cousins' children
Mom is with you now and you are no longer alone
August is fifty years since you left way too soon
It is time to celebrate you and what is

Toxicity

You put it to bed
You move on and forward
For good or bad doesn't matter you just do it
Then Friday the 13th comes and you get a call
Cemetery rates have risen
You have to step up to the plate again
No winners or trophies
You do the right thing again even though they didn't
You tuned into a better life while they tuned out
Happy that narcissism won't touch you again
You moved on with your adventure
Still walking in the rain

Banish Expectations

Plans have been tampered with and ushered out
the door
Celebrations and Milestones return to the back store
of your heart
Virtual everything just not cutting it any longer
Too much tension and despair, so that said, you have
to look deeper.
Try harder
People saying don't stress make it more difficult
What is small stuff to them is larger for you
Find a bit of magic every single day because for now
expectations and plans have to go away
Stash them with your dreams

Stay In Your Lane

Walking accompanied by doves and robins
Ease on down the road
Watch the syncopation of the rain
Gasp at March winds in April with May around
the corner
Be kind and caring but mind your business
Stay in your lane
Might not be the nicest way to put it but the world
is rotating strangely
Some people you wouldn't want to befriend
If you are lucky, you have a golden circle like mine

Extemporaneous

Not orchestrated
Sometimes impromptu
Off the cuff, but not usually
The impulse has been with me for as long as I can
remember
Hence keyboard, writing instrument, and paper always
nearby
At the ready
For to be the writer I dreamed
of being
Extemporaneously or not
The old school white or yellow legal pad seems to stare
at me
Until I grab for a pen and write
Or it grabs at me

You Had To Go And Be On Your Way

Unbelievable
Unthinkable
Waiting for you to call
Picked up the phone too many times
No long distance to Heaven
No visiting hours
We will tell your story
Share photographs and memories with your
great-grandchildren
Third Mother's Day without you
August will be three years since we bid you farewell
We wanted you to stay
So much more to do and say
You had to be on your way
Daddy was waiting for you
So were your parents and others we said goodbye to
You had to go and be on your way

Middle Class Philanthropist

Was going to use the word poor but for alliteration only
See there is nothing poor here
Just missed and for the time being that is the way it is
Somebody noticed that I give to charities and never
take anything for it
They give you free treats which others might want
or need
You only see the surface and never really know what
is going on in another's world
Wearing one of my beloved Care Bear masks, I heard
someone say she really is a human Care Bear
Still speechless, I am reminded that I am rich in family
and friends
My poetry always by my side
A lot of love and simple pleasures that make me
wealthy
Doing good makes me happy even now and always
You do the very best you can and sometimes more
when others are not looking

It Is Very Clear

Some, despite the need, refuse to learn
They don't think and stopped learning when school ended
School is not a building, in fact it is all around you
Reading is not only fundamental
It is as important as breathing
Communicating face to face or in a group is getting away from us
Technology lets us reach out but the contact is the reach in
You wonder why people talk at each other and not talk to each other
While we are at it
When was the last time you listened and not heard?
It is very clear
Or is it?

Naming It

Toxic people and environments in your own backyard
Co-dependents who enable without realizing why they
do it
Party to what they know and not what they don't
Just when the company of a pad, a pen and a keyboard
were allies
There is digital poetry to investigate and engage in
For what it is worth
Giving it a name starts the process

Outside Looking In

Not an oldies song though it is heard on Sirius radio.
When you love someone trying to run and ruin your life
You learn that you don't like them
Narcissistic tendencies don't make sense to the
sensitive and or creative types
Like those who read and teach Thoreau and hike
Walden Pond
When you have a connection and experience touching
Henry David's desk
Those who are different know the score
Now, you are inside looking out
No explanation should be necessary, as it were
As it is

New York Tough

Thanks Jerry Seinfeld
Thanks Andrew Cuomo
Make up your mind, Mr. Mayor
Whose side are you really on?
Mister President your press secretary compared
teachers to meat packers.
All important, but a lot more than apples and oranges
We are not babysitters and we have the education to
prove it.
It is so much more than making it through the rain or
the memory of 9/11.
What is essential to some doesn't matter to others
We have always had the right stuff
Even when good wasn't good enough
Whatever came at us we made it through
New York Tough
New York Tough

Looked Deeper Inside

If you don't care for and about yourself, what good
are you to your family and loved ones
Hard lesson learned when you are a giving and loving
person that puts themselves last most of the time
Looked deeper inside and made a little time for me
though it isn't easy for me

No Filter

Somebody crossed the line
Meant well but should have initiated brain and not
mouth
Just because you think of something, doesn't give you
the right to hurt somebody
Intention has nothing to do with it
Keep it to yourself
There are those out there with a mission to fix people
Take them as they are if you have a chance at
a friendship
That is a word that should never be given out randomly
or assigned without consideration
As does the word love
People with no filter need to keep their distance

No Need To Explain

You know me
Don't you?
Better than I know myself
What matters?
What makes me tick and tock?
Not the website
Being creative is not easy
Some don't understand
Somehow never needed to explain myself to you
You called me special and still do
You see a beauty that I don't see
Luckily, by the angels care and grace of the galaxy
You still love me and I love you
no need to explain
The couple still hand in hand will be us

Random Or Is It?

Delicate
Intricate
Unique
Creative
Conversations
Narratives
Repressed
Observed
Are these challenges?
Random
Even if they are not
What do you expect or should you?
Embrace them and enjoy
While you can and are able
Random
Luck
Just show them that you can do it and do it well
Random?

Rest In Love

Many said farewell
Part of life
Not like in 2020
As we grieve others do as well
There was no comfort we could provide
We could not visit
That hug that would say so much just was not possible
Every holiday and moment passes
You shed a tear and you remember
So that said
Rest In Love
You are not forgotten
Broken hearts mend but never heal completely

Seizing The Day Your Way

You don't want to be a cliche or live like one
Somewhere along the way when there are more thorns
than roses
You have to decide what you want for yourself
Used to think that was selfish but as the caring and
giving type
not so sure anymore
Kindness is something to strive for and is my nature
Lately, not sure if the good ones can seize the day
The members of that team are wiping tears away
hoping a smile will come through while trying to seize
the day
Listen very carefully
Digest
Then do your thing your way
Upside down
Downside up
Getting mixed messages
How much common sense and sense did we lose
in 2020?
Are we still losing?
Are you still arriving?
Are we writing the truth?
Find a balance between old school and new school
thinking
Getting lost in the shuffle
We are imbalanced as it is
Find your balance
Cervantes taught us that living passionately is the best
course to follow
As caring and as giving as you may very well be
Seize everyday passionately
Your very own way
Always find time to keep learning

Not Meant To Be

Yesterday was your birthday
Not stalking you, just revisited yesterday
Won't reach out and never will
Reminders of you are a very bitter pill
SUBO, Whitehead Hall, and Boylan came to call
It was long ago and far from away
Hope your life is happier today
It was not meant to be even for nineteen-year-old me
Was blind and deaf to reality, you see
Why you played along as a friend, history will show
Better things happened later there this is how it
would go
My husband and two master degrees came
Life has never been the same
We were not meant to be
Took a very long time to move forward you see
I wanted and needed you but all you could do was take
and not give
Not a life I wanted to live

Not The Way You Imagined

Together everything is easier
But it won't be easy
Find a way to make it look like it is
Especially when everybody is looking
Who really cares if they are talking because you can't
control what they think and say
They need to self-edit and self-control
Just know your heart and soul
There are surprises along with moments that will
become memories
You will reach for them when they are needed on rainy
and stormy days
Winter does come during the Summer, so be ready,
though you can never be sure but be sure of each other
Not the way you imagined but incredible just the same
Choose your love carefully and only be crazy for your
one and only

Cracked Mirror

What you see is a dream
It isn't there
It is not real
Even though you want it to be
You can't make somebody change when a message has
been branded into their heads by people who love them
conditionally
Children imprint messages and sometimes yesterday
never goes away
Despite your best efforts
She can't see the world through your eyes
She tried
Cracked mirror

Been There

Darkness was my only friend
My friends had no idea and maybe a clue
Even happily married because I had to find my way
back to him
He has been there every step of the way
Patience and help brought me through the storms
They still return but not as often
Walk them and write them away
Find ways to help others even though they might not
be aware that I care
You will find it
No matter what it is to soothe things
Asking for help, that was the most difficult part
Admitting something was more than off kilter
Even though I have been there
Just know it is different for everybody
Covid didn't help and it lingers
Been there and you fight gently

Here It Goes

Been there and been through turmoil and hell,
Buried things that should have exited long ago.
Wanted to protect someone who was too ill to help
His exit broke my spirit
My apologizes to my friends and loved ones who knew
about my anger all the time
You never threw your hands up, thanks
If you did, your loss
Took a caring physician to open the door to a very
dark world.
He did and made me work hard to change not just
who I am but why I am.
Even those who love you can't listen the way you need
them too.
So a professional with a trained ear was suggested and
the talk worked
People who are extra sensitive usually find a way in
this world and we still get stuck
Asking for help just isn't something we do
We want to help others but there comes a time when
you have to ask
The denim blue stormy days still come but they are far
and few between
You let go of those who hurt you
You surround yourself with the very best of people
If you have been bullied than you know what I mean
There are some here that qualify as the best and lucky
to call some here friends
Here it goes
Get what you need
Ask for help even if you are not confident enough
to do so
Realize that something needs to change and you start
the change

Seek it and don't leave us because you don't think there
is a way out
You have to go in and find a guide to help you
Here it goes and I hope you find it
It is more than fine to be a work in progress
Your life is not work, find a way to enjoy it
It is so much more than making lemonade from lemons

Open Your Heart

If you open your heart
The rest will follow
Surely as rainbows come after rainy days
Surely as you can wish upon a star
Take good care of yourself first
Guilty as charged because I put others before myself
Open your eyes
Close your mouth
Open your mind
Open your heart

How Do You Follow That?

The very best of the best
So special unlike the rest
One and only
One in a billion
I am talking about my one and only
How do you follow that?
How do you follow that?

Leo Sunshine

Did his smile warm you?
Did his blue eyes light up your life?
Chase the gray away
Hope for tomorrow and helping today
When he tells you at two and a half that he is special
Leo welcoming you into his world
The old soul in that little face
Leo Sunshine
Leo Sunshine
Leo Sunshine
It's how he tells you and the wonder around him
He takes you in and shares it with you
Leo Sunshine
Leo Sunshine
Leo Sunshine
Nobody could be so sublime
In this place and time
Like Leo Sunshine on my mind

Faded Stars

The sky is usually inviting even though the telescope
still isn't on my deck
Not tonight
Crying and writing don't usually go together but this
time they do
Photographs and memories will have to do but was
hoping for more time spent with you
One of the stars in my life who shone brightly has
dimmed
How lucky to have known you and played a part in
your life
More importantly we called each other friend.
So when I am able, looking for a shooting star or a
falling star hoping you know what you meant and will
always mean to me and many others

Heart Burn

How Will The Lessons Be Learned?

Of history
Of mystery
Of art
Of tradition
Of stories
Of legends
Of culture
Of music
Tell them
Share them
Talk and discuss
Face to face
Not online
Not on TikTok
Not texting
Word by word
Stories to be read, shared, passed down and
remembered
Cherished
This is how lessons should be learned

Months That End In Er

Beaches beckon come walk on my sand and share
my shore
Enjoy the rides and arcades
The crowds are gone so enjoy more
Enjoy summer just a little bit longer
Before the days grow shorter and darken
Indian Summer perhaps
September 11 brought attacks, challenges, adaptation,
adjustment and aftermath
Now recovery and redemption
Sorrow personified and magnified
We will never forget
We will always remember for DC, New York,
and Pennsylvania
Months that end in ER begin again and again
They never really end
They echo on our hearts

Out Of Left Field

When does one push the stop button?
When the noises in your head get so loud you stop
them before they explode
Leaving you to wonder do you leave well enough alone?
Just leave
Pick up the pieces and move forward
Is there anything left of what used to be?
Has the virus destroyed so much that all we do is
stand still
While others try another approach
Sweetness has been lost in the air

Hit Edit Button

Despite all good intentions
You may mean well
It is their life
Try listening with no comment or agenda
Their way of thinking
Their way of going through the motions or not
Think before you speak and hit the edit button

Inspire Yourself

Acquire
Aspire
Desire
Fire
If your fire goes out
Find a way to relight it
In between the heart break
Required
Retire to something you really want to accomplish
that you pushed aside
Inspire yourself
and others

You're Older

You're older but you are not old
They call you a boomer
So I have been told
Respect and honesty hasn't gone away
Kindness and caring is here to stay
It is a number on a birth certificate
Used to bes are in triplicate
Enjoy your life and live its bounty in stride
Be a participant and don't hide
Too many goods have been exchanged and sold
You're older but you're not old

Release And Move Forward

Say what you mean
Not what others say and think
Think very carefully before you regret what comes out
of your mouth
Quiet and silence sends powerful messages very well
There are many hellos and goodbyes in life
Dreams and fairytales come true and with that come
troubles
You revisit what works
You cast aside people when the friendship expiration
date can't be renewed
You will know the ones to hold on to because they will
always be there and vice versa
Just turn around
Be open to new friendships but learn from the past
Choose wisely before they choose you
Letting go and moving forward is not a cliche
You can't stay in neutral or in the past
That is just the way it is
You will find your way

Bullied

You are different
You don't look like them
You have nothing in common with them
They torture you with comments, giggles, and making
you feel as if you don't go with the flow
You can just go and be ignored
Parents and teachers told you to forget it and let it go
Easier said than done and kids can be cruel
It is their way or the highway
So lunchtime you sat alone
Read and did your homework
Your best friend was writing and poetry
Same holds true today
Difference is I don't take CRAP from anyone
Haven't got time for the those who don't know how
to be kind and caring
Princesses and Princes of the world male and female,
yes you.

Is It Too Much to Ask?

Is it too much to ask to be entertained?
Creative arts
Performing arts
Conversation
Nature
Enjoying life
There is a time and place for news and information
Are we on overload?
Have we been drained of curiosity and wonder?
Did we shut down and shut off?
What have we lost?
What have we gained?
Have we changed so much that what enjoyed is lost
forever?
We have lost our patience in the everyday task of living
Is it too much to ask to be better than we used to be

Are We Going Together?

Is that all there is?
There is nothing more to say?
Nothing to look forward to?
Nothing to share or plan?
Are you trapped in your head?
On too loosely or tightly?
Stuck in neutral?
Is the silence too deafening to you?
Where do we go from here?
Is a there available?
Click and tick of the computer keyboard or cell phone
Where do we go from here?
Are we going together?
Please don't tell me you abide by the words and deeds
of Mr. Despicable Narcissist?

What Matters

People and places
Friends old and new
Some waiting to meet in person
Shooting the breeze and connecting
Face to face
Person to person
Concentrate on what pleases you and those around you
Let go of what and who wastes your time
Learned the hard way that loss changes more than time
and place
Memories only hold on to yesterday
Still cherish them
What matters most is now and tomorrow
Remember today

For A Very Long Instant

I caught you looking at me
This time I caught your glance and returned that stare
Eighteen and nineteen were long ago
The scar is there
You can let things go but some memories burn and
destroy your spirit
See you move on with an attitude but now it is
of gratitude
He showed me the way
A life quite remarkable
You accept not expect
You don't need a lot to be a Prince Charming or to be
swept up by one
All it takes is to be loved for the human being that
you are
For a very long instant and daily
I treasure what I have and what I learned
He is an original and despite the hurdles we
currently face
Together we can conquer it all

Talking To A Stone

Mom's unveiling was almost a year ago
All I could do was hug your monument at the cemetery
Didn't want to let go
Hate visiting there
You should know that because other than once you
visited a cemetery
You never returned as far as I know
You have missed so much and I miss you more than
any poetry books I will write
Daddy, I am published
The tears are falling harder this year because your 95th
birthday just passed and we can't celebrate or spoil you
Taken from us far too soon fifty years ago when
you were
Forty-five
Still need a community to be a writer
Thought I found it but still unsure
A platform for exchange is needed but not my decision
or choice
You taught me never to believe or use the words I can't
in a sentence or in my mind
Still sometimes that fifteen-year-old girl still talking
to a stone
Hoping you hear me because her father died from
a heart attack as she watched it happen
That little gray dove on the railing this morning sat
there as if it was hugging me and
drying my tears
Was it you?

Curve Ball

You can be devoted
You can be kind
You can be considerate
You can be loyal and true
Then a curve ball is thrown to upset the apple cart
Learn how to catch it
Better still, throw your own and redirect it

Heart Songs

Three More Mondays

You see your world flash through your mind
As you wipe the tears away in the shower so he
won't see
Watching him in pain is heart breaking
You learn how much you love someone and you
battle together
Hoping this never happens again but you can never
say never
It's a six letter word that turns whatever you knew
inside out and upside down
It's not a been there done that situation
Dollar bills blind the cure
Three more Mondays and we bid cancer farewell
Hoping it stays clear of family and friends
Three more Mondays

Lunch With Squirrels

They sat on two branches
One above the other
Adorable as could be
Gathered bits of cantaloupe, nuts, and cookies
into a cup
Found the tree and called out to them
Scattered the food all around the tree
They sat on their branches enjoying
Made an ordinary lunch extraordinary

Ringing The Bell

For beginnings and endings
For excelsior, onward and upward
For honoring and remembering
For new stars in the galaxy
For marking time and place
Ring them long and loud
Ring them strong and clear
Ring them as you mark your personal victory as
a survivor
Ring them so friends and family can cheer
Ring the bell and and let the chime carry you through
So you do the very best you can and more than you
thought you were capable of
Ring the bell and listen

Painting Words

Are you seeking the correct word or words?
Imagery
Photographs and landscapes
Colors Crayola has not conceived of yet
Do they tell the story?
Is it fresh and new?
Does it capture what you need it to say?
Is your muse beckoning you?
Did they wake you again in time to type it or jot it
down?
In the middle of the night
Just when sleep comes
You know you are no longer a novice
You are a writer being called to do what you must do
Pleasant dreams and hope your passion keeps your
poetry coming

Can I Love You Better?

How can it be stronger?
I have no clue
Been with you almost all of my adult life
We found each other when we least expected it
No matter what life throws at us
Or graciously bestows upon us
There is nothing short of a felony because that is
not me
That I would not do for and because of you
No Herculean task would be too great
Can I love you any better?
I doubt it
You know stopping me would involve jumping
over galaxies
I love you more than I even know
Better

Please Stop Thanking Me

You placed a band of gold on my finger
Your ring matches exactly
We share our lives together
I love you beyond measure and if ever they measure
that it wouldn't be large enough or high enough
Please stop thanking me
Thank you

You Found Me

Wasn't looking long ago
He stepped on my heart
That Italian Stallion sat on my soul
Wasn't looking and you found me
In the middle of the night the blue eyes catch me
sleeping
Gently cover you making sure pleasant dreams
surround you
Best friend and love of my life
Glad you found me and you love me

Iced Tea And Biscotti

Tea is my favorite beverage and iced is the delight
Biscotti or Mandel Bread seems to be the perfect
partner
This breakfast started for me in Florence, Italy
Espressos and Lattes surrounded me, yet there was
a tall frosted glass
That was every day in Italy and sometimes at home
Have teas from all over the world and enjoy Harney's
Teas
Passion fruit delights me
Sometimes my writing companion because it is easy
and free
Weather permitting, I bake my own for that is a
quiet joy
Iced Tea and Biscotti
Cheers

Now Not Yesterday

You love who you love
No country or government should dictate otherwise
No religion
No political party
Nor should any state or country tell women how
to live their lives.
As a straight women who survived a crime and am
forever changed and scarred by it, how dare they!
LGBQT people deserve respect
Think what you want but be kind and thoughtful
Now, not yesterday

Better Days Ahead

The alarm went off again
Another repeat and routine
Necessary evil
The WORST part of the marriage vows
You are the one to see your love through
The treatment commercials make their point
Just once show both sides of the story
You hate cancer and you want to rid the earth of it
Treating it is one thing
Watching your loved one and yourself deal is quite
another
Deal, you will
Places to go and people to see
Ringing that bell and he will
It is so much more than ringing the bell
Better days ahead

It's Your Time

No reason
No rhyme
May not come tomorrow
May not come today
You're on your way
So much for you to do
Not too much to say
A lot more than trying
It's living completely not dying

Trompe L'Oeil

Gris and Picasso both
fool and train the eye with images magnificently
They make words pop
They play with the eye
It's different shades and takes on a world some just
don't see even if they are looking
As a visual learner and a writer, it captures a place
I hold dear
Sometimes what stands out holds itself to a higher
plane because the music of the heart and soul falls into
the hands of those that impact the world in a way few
imagine and a special few accept
Trompe l'oeil
Trompantojo

Italy

She beckons me to return
Something changed when the words work to live
became a mantra
Celebrating friends and family with a joy never known
before
Just because and a dolce vita state of mind
You enjoy and take out the good stemware and stuff for
special occasions every day
You make every moment a holiday because indeed it is
a gift to be here and enjoy
That is the reason
So until we meet again dear lovely cities
Your art and culture never stop filling my cup
Firenze look for me
Venezia your magic fills the air
Italy with a style and colors of its own
A tutto c'e' rimecho fuorche la morta
Arrivederci alla prossimo

Only Walking In The Rain

Expectations not so much
Dreams to be conquered and enjoyed until new ones
appear
Wet circles big and small syncopated as the umbrella
plays pizzicato
as you try to stay dry
Damp and dreary for some
Invigorating for others
Leaving Starbucks with last sip of black iced tea in hand
Only walking in the rain

Rainy Days And Mondays No Longer Get Me Down

Rainy days and Mondays no longer get me down
Sorry Richard and the late Karen Carpenter
Snow and ice get me down
They are pretty but get in the way and are hazardous
Sorry skiers and skaters
Naysayers may not apply or get in the way of what matters
What matters is doing the very best possible
Doing the right thing when the wrong thing is easier
A taste
that completely disagrees with me
My heart is on a page and one that I author
Some will never open it
Too much has happened
Too many last said goodbyes
Rainy days and Mondays no longer get me down

Heart Strings

Pooh

The face
That sweet and honest face
Makes me happy still long after I was three
He is always around me
No matter where I go or what I do
Pooh I will always love you
Then and now until this khaki coil isn't under my feet.
Pooh, it is you, my sweet

Nature's Song

Henry David taught me well
Hiking on Walden Pond brought it forward
Nature and her children sing and frolic
The thunder and lightning and storms worn us
she is a force to be reckoned with
Enjoy the sky, the wind,
waterways, oceans, predators and prey
As you sit in awe and enjoy the vistas and bounty
Remember we should care, protect, and respect
everything around us
Not only should you sing her songs
Stand up and stand by her always

Before You Say I Love You

It is a four letter word
Sometimes over said
Sometimes a green light for a one night stand
You are not in it to fix someone
You take them as they are
If not, get on your way
Sometimes what you are looking for becomes what
you never expected
Usually better than you ever dreamed of
Perhaps expectations are not warranted
You can fall into like
You can fall into lust
Keep your raging hormones in check
Say those words to your one and only
Before you say I love you, there are too many one way
streets with dead ends
You walk down one and you never come back again

Swan Song

You have done your utmost
Somehow that is enough for others
Maybe you have done it all and time to move on?
Why hang in when you are not wanted
Or feel like a used to be
Been made to feel like something or place had
to be created for you
Just to stay?
Take your bow
Say farewell and amen
Knowing in your heart you will find other places to
be useful
When right now, you feel useless though you did it
your way

Extreme Care

Editing is not just for writing
It is for speaking
It is for dignity, honor, and respect
It is for being human
Say what you want but watch how and where you say it
Social media has hurt people
Words hurt people even though we try our best
Sometimes that isn't even enough
Extreme care
Everywhere
Please don't make promises you can't keep

Reimagination

Everything old is new again
Refreshed and updated for now
Remembering and cherishing what was, what is and
what will be
Without what was, getting to the future will be difficult,
but we must celebrate now
Sure there are repeats and relics
Oldies and newbies
Creation and innovation
We hear you
Reimagination goes nowhere without respect for
the past
We can't live in it but we must acknowledge and
appreciate it
Without history
Where would we be?
Reimagination is in the heart and head where creativity
Dwells

Other Side Of The Rainbow

Been a rainbow chaser my entire life
There are dark hours all around us
We will break through and find a way to the dawn as we
salute all those heroes and heroines out there
doing their utmost to get us through
It will be worth it in the end, but there is a lot of grief
and sorrow accompanying all of us
Make a difference every single day
You will decide and make us all proud
We can't look the other way
Those literal ones out there may not get it
Us figurative types have it, always have
We never fit in before, but we do now and forevermore
in better days ahead

Carousel

Finally got that brass ring
All the other times just wanted to set you free and go
galloping
The beautiful artwork and craftmanship from
Coney Island to both US coasts always caught my eye
Still ride you wherever I am but enjoy how incredible
regal you are
Ridden horses before but nothing compares with the
ride I take with you and that music
Amazing organs not the ones that are recorded
Love carousels
Up down and around

Moments To Cherish

Bird fluttering by my window
Squirrel stopping to look my way after feasting on nuts
and treats left by the tree
Our two-year-old niece being kissed by a nine-week-old
puppy to her delight
Walking hand and hand with our nieces grown and
small
Awe, sigh, and grateful moments

Diamond In The Rough (Lyrics)

He's a breath of fresh air
All that and devil may care
Never seen a complete package like him before
Looked up and he walked through the door

Chorus
He's a diamond in the rough
He's the bomb and all the right stuff
More than enough, the dude is tough
Never seen a dream come true
Better for me and not for you

When you stop looking you'll be found
Somebody makes your world spin right side up
and upside down
Repeat first four lines
Chorus and then fade

If You Fall Asleep In My Arms

If you fall asleep in my arms
Rocked ever so gently
Letting go of what is over
Holding on to promises kept and memories yet to
be fulfilled
We will make more
Making sure that darkness will soothe you and the stars
will be a night light
Letting you dream peacefully and comfortably
We can only move forward now
What was is over
Not looking back
Just want you to rest, recover and sleep easily
Love you, but not loving you tonight or in the near
future until you are ready again
Remember how we arrived here and where we have
yet to go
If you fall in my arms
Pleasant dreams because the nightmare is over and
in check
If you fall asleep in my arms

Beech Trees

Watch the rain glisten on the yellow leaves as the
sun tries to come out
Even on the windiest and colder days in
December her leaves are full of sunshine
Every shade of yellow but lemony and lovely
As you watch the rain circles near the ducks in the pond
The warmer days of December come back to your
memories
As the cities come back to life with visitors
As Christmas, Kwanza, and Chanukah celebrations
take their shape
The Beech tree kept me company and happy on a lonely
December day
Reminding me of better days to come

Grandpa's Girl

He died before I was born.
Seen old photos but they didn't speak much of him.
Like family lore some stories conflict.
He liked to cook and so do I
Squirrels sat on his shoulders and ate nuts from his
hands and pockets.
I never get that close but once a week when time
permits they get fresh roasted unsalted nuts.
Sometimes they look my way as if to say thanks.
Never knew him but somehow, named after him.
I am Grandpa's girl

The Little Brook

Why had I not noticed this sweet little waterway
before?
I crossed the street and never stopped to notice
Will rectify that as I usually do notice
Just for a few moments took a breath as the rain
stopped
The clouds parted, and the sky started to turn blue
Because of you little brook

Overhearing Gris And Picasso

How many guitars did you capture?
Chiaroscuro worked well for some
Did you enjoy the colors you employed?
To be a fly on the wall during that conversation
Picasso shared that artists lie and truth is not their goal
Perhaps it is a truth at many different levels
Neither Pablo nor Juan is still here for us to ask
Can you imagine that conversation if they were?

Moving Forward

Indefatigable defines me and many others in
different ways
Comfortable in my skin now
Respecting myself and others
You don't take yourself seriously but you take
seriously what you do
The way you live in this world
Sometimes listening very carefully works wonders
So does keeping still and taking it all in
Moving forward that is what's planned
Finding time to sit in parks or beaches
Feeding squirrels and wildlife
Letting it all go by with great appreciation and respect

Knowing Your Heart

How it beats
Who it beats for
Your passion
Your strength
How to treat it when it heals and breaks
Remember wounds that run deep
Knowing your heart and my love goes with you

Without You

You kept me entertained on many stormy days in
my life recently
Talking didn't help me
Your acrobatics and sweet way of moving about would
warm anyone's soul as long as they keep their distance
You are cute and sweet with shades of blue, white,
black and silver and gray
Love nuts and fruit accepting what humans leave
for you
On days when crying was all I could do without you
a smile would never come to my face

The R's Of Life

Respect
Reverence
Responsibility
Reality

Parade Of Planets

At daybreak
On the east coast of the United States
Take a closer look
Mercury, Saturn, and Venus
Crescent moon
A parade of planets

Troubles And Triumphs

Happy July
Somehow we made it despite and in spite of what is out
of our control
Cancellations, hurdles, rescheduling and need for more
patience
Reflect all that you want to
Giving up isn't an option
Nor is running out or moving away
Complain until you turn another's ears blue
Take peaceful and gentle action
Quietly and affirmatively in a group
Jump through hurdles with a plan
Be selective and careful
As we continue our troubles and triumphs
Looking for a double rainbow in the sky
Oh my

Calm Before The Storm

The bread would be fresh for two more days and
we were not finishing it
Thought of the bluebirds that gave me such joy
Quickly cut the remainder up and walked to the park
One bluebird was perched on a high branch
Sparrows had their daily meeting on the ground
A sparrow was walking around because a feral cat
was around
He sent the warning chirp
The bread was placed there and by a big tree
As I walked away the bread was happily devoured
and no sign of the poor cat
Many people feed the feral cats but didn't want those
cats making meals of the birds or squirrels
Calm before the storm

P Words

Phenomenal
Poetic
Positive
Precious
Passionate
Proper
Piquant
Purpose
Puzzling
319 adjectives start with the letter P
Do you have a favorite?

September Rain Song

Monarch butterflies are nowhere to be found
Lovely but dangerous lantern flies are hiding
No jumping today
Squirrels are taking a nap
Birds flew away into higher trees
Count the small wet rings that become large circles
Like the chorus
Melody and harmony is soft but you can sing along
Altos and sopranos
This one is for you
The light gray cloudy sky turning to an angry dark gray
with a patch of black
The syncopation, harmony, melody and rhythm are all
here in the September rain song

For Dara

She talks of affection
She talks of loss
She talks of angels here on earth
She tells of stories others can share
Battles that keep happening
Soldiers who will fight for a win
Tee shirts with names of those who suffered
They are remembered with love and joy
She will not rest until esophageal cancer has a cure and
treatment
The fourth annual walk today proves her spirit and
determination with many cheering her on
Congratulations to her and to all that walked and
participated
See you next year
Looking forward to progress and good news

To Be That Seagull

Meow
HEHO HEHO
Huoh-Huoh
Listen to them
My dad would name them as they scooped food out
of the unknowing hands of people on boardwalks
Flying over the blues and waves of the beach and
the shore
How much can we learn from them?
Sometimes I am envious of their lives
They touch the blues of the skies and the light
To be that seagull flying high

Poet's Walk

Cleansing and therapeutic
A butterfly and three ducks for company
Two black and white marbled
The other marbled with a touch of red near her head
My spirit animals a bear and swan always with me
The very best company
The golden butterfly landed near me on a water break
All on a Poet's Walk

Flying High

Muscovy ducks swimming in a pond
Others sunning themselves under the bushes so they
are protected from the sun's rays
Pomeranian and Swedish blues enjoying the breezes
Squirrels of many colors and shades competing for
taller branches and edible delights

My Body My Life

Whatever your religious thoughts are
They are respected and understood
As well as your feelings
Please see other side for a moment
If your life is at stake
If you have survived an attack and I speak from my
experience only
Where my body and life were forever changed
Years of therapy and dealing with Depression was
the price and telling my beloved what happened
before we embarked to what will be 43 year marriage
this autumn
Wanted children but a rapist took that from me
at fourteen
If you acted first and thought better later
If your partner was not prepared for the situation
after the fact
If you are not ready financially, emotionally, or
whatever the reason
My body, my life, my choice
The medication and right to choose is not a **state's** nor
judge's decision
As for Florida and other states that have banned
the choice
There are no words just tears

Acknowledgements

Thanks to Cheryl and The Three Tomatoes

In Memory of Manuel Epstein, my father
In Memory of our friend Dr. Leni Kramer

About the Author

Madlyn Epstein Steinhart has been writing poetry since the age of eight. It gave her an internal voice when she felt powerless to speak out. Madlyn is a retired New York City public school teacher, a grant writer, and a media literacy specialist. This is her second collection of poetry. Her debut collection is titled, *Put Your Boots on and Dance in the Rain.*

www.ingramcontent.com/pod-product-compliance
Lightning Source LLC
Chambersburg PA
CBHW060239030426
42335CB00014B/1527